The Night Walk

written by Jennifer Jacobson • illustrated by Maryjane Begin

HARCOURT BRACE & COMPANY

Orlando Atlanta Austin Boston San Francisco Chicago Dallas New York
Toronto London

I am going on a night walk.

What's behind this log?
It's a toad. A hopping brown toad.
I might keep him.

What's on this leaf?
It's a bug. A light-up-the-night bug.
I might keep him.

What's up in the air?
It's a moth. A high-flying moth.
I might keep him.

It's time to go inside.
What's under here?

Not a hopping brown toad.
Not a light-up-the night bug.
Not a high-flying moth.

It's a sleepy spotted lizard.
I'll take good care of you!